IT'S TIME TO LEARN ABOUT COYOTES

It's Time to Learn about Coyotes

Walter the Educator

Silent King Books
A WhichHead Entertainment Imprint

Copyright © 2025 by Walter the Educator

All rights reserved. No part of this book may be reproduced in any manner whatsoever without written per- mission except in the case of brief quotations embodied in critical articles and reviews.

First Printing, 2024

Disclaimer

This book is a literary work; the story is not about specific persons, locations, situations, and/or circumstances unless mentioned in a historical context. Any resemblance to real persons, locations, situations, and/or circumstances is coincidental. This book is for entertainment and informational purposes only. The author and publisher offer this information without warranties expressed or implied. No matter the grounds, neither the author nor the publisher will be accountable for any losses, injuries, or other damages caused by the reader's use of this book. The use of this book acknowledges an understanding and acceptance of this disclaimer.

It's Time to Learn about Coyotes is a collectible early learning book by Walter the Educator suitable for all ages belonging to Walter the Educator's Time to Eat Book Series. Collect more books at WaltertheEducator.com

USE THE EXTRA SPACE TO TAKE NOTES AND DOCUMENT YOUR MEMORIES

COYOTES

The coyote lives both near and far,

It's Time to Learn about

Coyotes

In deserts wide or under star.

From grassy plains to forest deep,

It hunts and plays, then goes to sleep.

It looks a bit like cousin dog,

With pointy ears and paws that jog.

Its fur is brown or gray or tan,

It's built to run, just like a van!

Coyotes howl beneath the moon,

A high-pitched song, a lonely tune.

They talk this way to say, "I'm here!"

To other coyotes far and near.

They're hunters, yes, but clever too,

They know just what they need to do.

They chase down mice or rabbits fast,

And eat their meals until the last!

It's Time to Learn about

Coyotes

Sometimes alone, sometimes in pairs,

They sneak through fields and down the stairs

(Well, not real stairs, but canyon steep!)

Where lizards run and crickets leap.

They're not too big, they're not too small,

Just knee-high tall, that's about all.

But don't be fooled by what you see,

They're quick and smart and wild and free!

Coyotes live near people too,

In parks and towns and places new.

They look for food both day and night,

But try to hide and stay from sight.

They care a lot about their pack,

They'll help each other watch their back.

They raise their pups with love and pride,

It's Time to Learn about

Coyotes

And teach them how to run and hide.

If you should hear a yip or call,

Or spot one near a garden wall,

Be calm and quiet, let them be

They're just a part of Earth, like me!

So now you know this clever friend,

From pointy nose to tail's end.

The coyote's wild, strong, and true

It's Time to Learn about

Coyotes

From pointy nose to tail's end.

The coyote's wild, strong, and true

It's Time to Learn about

Coyotes

A special creature through and through!

ABOUT THE CREATOR

Walter the Educator is one of the pseudonyms for Walter Anderson. Formally educated in Chemistry, Business, and Education, he is an educator, an author, a diverse entrepreneur, and he is the son of a disabled war veteran. "Walter the Educator" shares his time between educating and creating. He holds interests and owns several creative projects that entertain, enlighten, enhance, and educate, hoping to inspire and motivate you. Follow, find new works, and stay up to date with Walter the Educator™

at WaltertheEducator.com

www.ingramcontent.com/pod-product-compliance
Lightning Source LLC
LaVergne TN
LVHW051920060526
838201LV00060B/4099